BABIES ON THE GO

Linda Ashman   ILLUSTRATED BY Jane Dyer

Editorial Offices: Glenview, Illinois • Parsippany, New Jersey • New York, New York
Sales Offices: Needham, Massachusetts • Duluth, Georgia • Glenview, Illinois • Coppell, Texas • Sacramento, California • Mesa, Arizona

Babies on the Go, text copyright © 2003 by Linda Ashman, Illustrations copyright © 2003 by Jane Dyer, reproduced by permission of Harcourt, Inc.

Big Book version of *Babies on the Go* published by Scott Foresman.

ISBN: 0-328-16878-5

1 2 3 4 5 6 7 8 9 10 V008 12 11 10 09 08 07 06 05

For Uncle Arthur and Aunt Jackie, with love—*L. A.*

For my friends Eric and Bobbie Carle—*J. D.*

Some babies stand up right away.

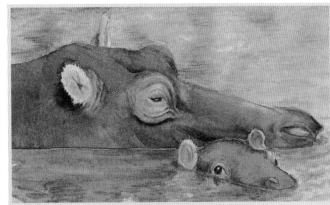

They take a step, then run and play.

5

But many need more time to grow,

6

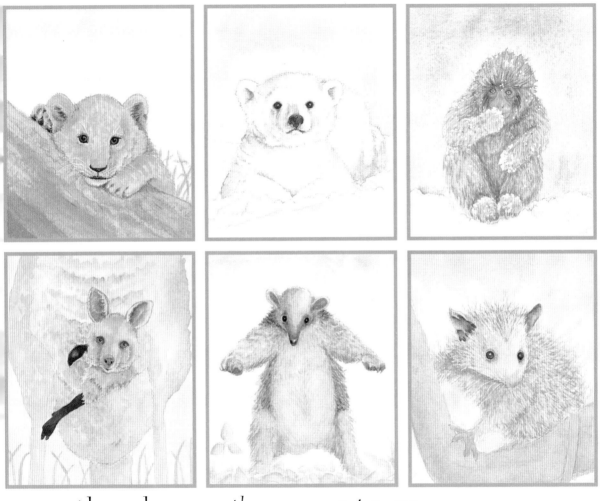

so they have *other* ways to go. . . .

8 Rolling by in baby strollers.

Holding tight to Mother's shoulders.

Grabbing on to clumps of hair.

Riding bareback through the air.

12   Swinging in a belly sling.

Sailing snug beneath a wing.

Towed along a bumpy trail.

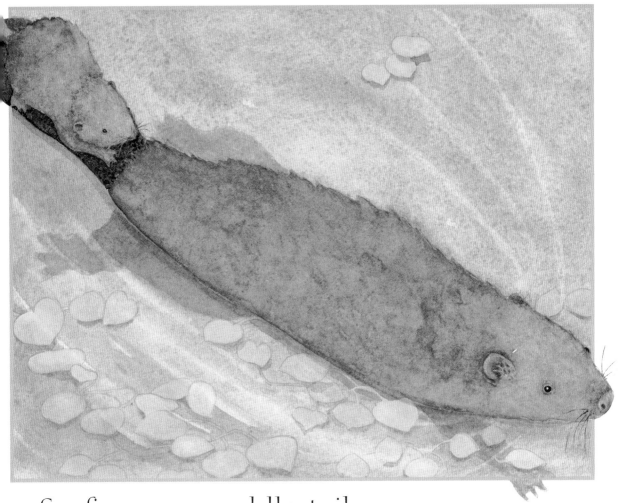

Surfing on a paddle-tail.

Flying by beneath a cape.

Dangling from a fuzzy nape.

Nudged along with gentle paws.

Floating by in giant jaws.

Perching on a mother's hip.

Stretching out on board a ship.

Tucked inside a private sack.

Boosted by a piggyback.

Touring solo on their ride.

Squeezed together, side by side.

It doesn't matter how they go.

Inside . . . outside . . . fast . . . or slow.

On the ground

or high above,

29

babies always ride with love.

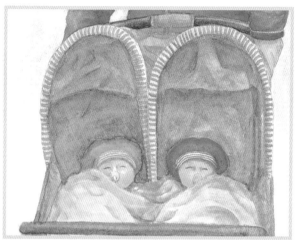
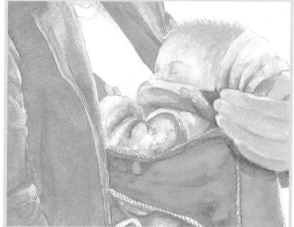

31

Meet the Babies

giraffe

deer

hippopotamus

koala

chimpanzee

monkey

sloth

swan

elephant

beaver

bat

lion

polar bear

crocodile

snow monkey

otter

kangaroo

lizard

anteater

opossum